TAKE ANY
SHIP THAT SAILS

TAKE ANY
SHIP THAT SAILS

MICHELE HEENEY

ARPress
ILLUMINATING IDEAS.
EMPOWERING VOICES

ARPress
45 Dan Road Suite 5
Canton MA 02021

Hotline: 1(888) 821-0229
Fax: 1(508) 545-7580

Ordering Information:
Quantity sales. Special discounts are available on quantity purchases by corporations, associations, and others. For details, contact the publisher at the address above.

Printed in the United States of America.

ISBN-13:	Softcover	979-8-89356-349-8
	Hardcover	979-8-89356-351-1
	eBook	979-8-89356-350-4

Library of Congress Control Number: 2024906346

Table of Contents

TIME

Uncharted

My conscious mind
Has its own
Unconscious mind
That rests
On a dark
Uncharted island
That floats on a
Collective universal
Sea

Blown about
By hot winds
Born of primordial
Time
Long before
My mind
Met its mind
Or this
Mind-filled body.

Tomorrow

We are day-eaters all,
Gluttons of time,
Mindlessly taking in
Morsels of moments
That will be served
But once.

Tomorrow we'll drink
A bitter brew
Of stale regrets
To clear our mouths
And minds
Of half tasted
Yesterdays.

Time

Willowy aftermath
  Of half remembered dreams,

Gossamer mist dividing
Today from forever.

We watch our hours
From a door beyond

And pass through
In silken slippers..

Two Thieves

Age takes youth
Death takes more.
Age dusts the windows
Death shuts the door.

Age takes beauty
Death, hope of spring.
Age take laughter
Death, everything.

Age steals thoughts
And times once known.
Age takes memories
Death leaves its own.

Age knows good times
Death knows none.
Age takes many
Death, everyone..

Wild Horses

Where are all those wild young horses
That sped across my landscape?
With flashing hooves and blood red eyes,
With steaming .esh and panting breath,
They tore through tender land,
Kicked up soul and sinew.

Led by one young stallion,
Passion was his name
Passion was his life,
Freedom followed at his neck
Across my fresh green earth.

So wild, so huge, so free they ran
With many more behind them.
Through white of day
Through black of night,
Up hills of wonder
Down valleys of regret
They stopped for none
Nor knew a master.

Now, I only hear their echo,
Feel the last of shaking earth.
They're all but gone,
Riding toward another golden sun,
Another promised land
While I must stay
To taste the dust of mine..

Shiva Speaks

Look to the sky.
No beginning
No end.

Beyond the edge
Of the universe,
My home.
No borders
No boundaries
Only infinity.

For me
Time is
A circle.
No first
No last
But Always.

I was
Before eternity
I will be
After eternity.

Contemplating
Space and time
Brings you closer
To me.

Come closer.

Trapped

We are all born free.
    Soon, time comes stalking
    The net drops down.

Tender minds,
    Tender flesh
    Ensnared

Sins recorded,
    Runaways captured.

    Trapped

Trapped,
    Then thrown
    To shadows.

Long before we die,
    We are ghosts.

Grey ghosts
    Condemned to haunt
    The few
    Who got away.

ART

The Art of Wine

Decanting rare wine
  From spent hours with

Lingering echoes
  Of memory.

Uncork the bottle,
  Strange music flows out,

Shards of mementos,
  Bits of the past.

While the measure of time
  Continues distilling
  A jug of bitter dross

Into a wine
  Too rich to drink..

Transformation

The small poet
Takes the fine pen
To probe thin nerves
Of invisible emotion
Causing liquid tears
To evaporate
Into transparent air

And the whole world
Shifts.

Shadow Side

Where is my dark poet,
The seeker of shadows,
The reader of dreams?

Where is my night angel
Who watches at evening
As the blackbird sleeps,

Knows where the rabbits run
As the night hawk hunts,
How the river holds the moonlight?

Where is my secret self
Who flashes golden spurs
At dawn?

Then gone.

Poetry

When writing
As with living
It's often best
To be still,
To wait,
To listen
For the right words
The right meaning
That lives not
In the mind
But in the bones.

When lost in confusion,
Leaning too close
To logic,
Trust that the light
Will find you,
That mystery will
Solve itself.

Trust in fruition
Where beauty and form
Will materialize
From a deeper,
Untamed region.

Pushing, pulling,
Beating on the door
Leads us
Off the scent,
Where only
Stillness and letting go
Will see us home..

Lady Art

Often wears
A filmy wrap
That veils
Her hidden meaning.

Yet, through
A tiny pinhole
In her gown
The artists
Inner spark
Is sought
And found,

A moment more
The pinhole's
Doubly sewn.
Yet, for one
Speck of time
The sensual form
Is fully known..

NATURE

Carmel Valley

That restless
Soul of mine
Finally slipped
Its silver anchor
Over the side,

Deep into that
Green and golden
Patch of earth.

I, of course,
Kept roaming
Through other
Charming lands

While my soul,
Still tethered
To the anchor,
Stayed..

El Rio Grande

Clouds alive
With mist
and wind

Dance through
The branches
Of old cottonwoods.

The Rio Grande
Caresses their reflection.

A scattershot
Of swallows
Blows about
Like bursts
Of black confetti.

The banks
That holds the river
Breathe silent prayers
Of stillness,

As the river sings
Her autumn song..

Mount Tamalpais

Weary of wishing
Soft lay me down
Spent of ambition
On your cool ground.

High mother mountain
On you I rest,
Peace from you fountain
I drink from your breast.

Cradle me sweetly
As I sleep by your streams
Humbly I seek thee
To nourish old dreams..

Michele Heeney

Monterrey Summer

Heart-breakable star drenched sky
Velvet black in deep July,
My blood turns to honey wine.

Warmed by the breath
Of ocean winds that drift
Through tall and flaxen wheat
On waves of summer heat.

Our skin turns pink, then peach, then tan,
Sweet apricot juice stains
My shirt and hand
1%ile you hair is blown about
Like wild com silk in the breeze.

Sweet July and August
Run together and soon
We feel as young as any
Yearling doe beneath the moon
Grazing on fallen plums at night.

All but forgotten
Cold February's chill,
Month of brittle bones,
Of frozen dawns
Without the bright warm sun's good will.

Stay, O swee July.
Please linger long.
Too soon comes the weight
Of winter's crushing wheel
When wine tums again to blood,
As bones turn to steel..

New Mexico

Raw west winds
Sweep across
Wide mesas,
Exquisite sky,
The canopy.

Willful spirits
Rip through
Troops of juniper.
Only the deeply rooted
Stand.

All else
Long, long since
Blown away.

To the pleasure
Of the desert gods
Coyotes sing
Their crazy love song
To this fearsome beauty.

Such is my interior canvas;
A wide, clean-swept soul scape
In pale earth tones.

Yet, sometimes
In deepest sleep
I dream of cool,
Moist nights,
Soft mist rising
Off verdant fields.

How could I not?
When celtic rain runs with
Ancient memories
Through my blood..

To Men of Progress

Please don't
Blow up
The moon.

We have
Grown quite
Fond of her.

The tides
Of oceans,
The tides
Of our bodies,
Have fallen in love
With her magic
Push and pull.

In love with
Her light in
The night sky,
Her hope in
Darkness and foreboding,
Her play of
Form and change.

She is
The silver pendant
The ancients
Have passed down.

Fool Moon

This big full moon
With its neon grin
Takes me by the throat
Lets the night witch in.

This blue full moon
Takes a hold of me
Won't set me free
Till the end of night.

That bright orb hanging
Keeps my brains clanging
Gets strange ghosts banging
Like some old barn doors.

This cool moon glow
With its ice blue light
Has its grip on me
Till the last of night.

Till dawn.

Leave the moon
To her eternal birth.
Haven't you done enough
To earth?.

LOVE

La Bebida Especial

When it comes to love
I sometimes find
A small sip of poison
Is just as fine
As a big, full glass
Of the best French wine.

Live Wire Fence

Had I only known one
Touch would send shots of
Lightening though my bones,
My heart, my skin,
So sharp, so deep, a bolt
Of raw electric

To scorch my body up and down
Singe my hair, my upper
Lip, burn holes in my socks,
My shoes, searing through the
Floor, into the cellar.

Had I only thought one
Touch could blind my eyes so
They could not see the present,
Bum my ears so
They could not hear the now
Leaving me stuck, staring
At the past.

What once was tranquil is
Burnt to ashes by the heat.
Still, after all this carnage
I want another touch..

To Run Alone

I am too responsible of late
Keeping my needs, my hopes
Behind a heavy gate,
Sending Wonder Girl to run about
Shutting pain and feelings out.

Once in a while my heart breaks
Through the ice
Of that cold, grey lake
It's drown in twice,
Stings me with its hot reality;
You with your love
Are not here with me.

I run alone so well it just seems right
To give my all on this long, low, solo fight.
But since you've touched me with your face
It seems now a sad, a sorry race-

To run alone..

Love Song

A flutter of emotion
Then sudden flight
On frantic wings.

Freed
From a twice lock cage
My heart went flying

To sing silent
Notes of hope
Upon your window sill..

Celibacy

When I knew for certain
No man would soon be near,
I took the angels on.

In that coupling
My heart blew open.
Then beauty,
That had been a stranger to me,

Poured forth
Like golden waterfalls..

Catch Me

Catch me.
Don't let me win this game.
Use your nest net,
Employ your fastest yacht,
Please you really ought
To catch me.

Grab me by the hand
Demand I understand
I'm running out of time.
Lock me in your arms.
Catch me.

If I don't stop soon
I'll crash into the moon
Out in cold dark space.
What a crazy race!

If it seems the clouds I seek
It's not. I'm just too weak
To cease this silly game.
What I truly need
Is an end to all this speed.

So if while gazing at the sky
You see me flying by,
Kiss me on the mouth

And catch me.

Standing At Your Door

I once had
A blood red heart.
It sang
It soar,
It sailed.

Now it's stuck
To the sole
Of your shoe.

Now there's a hole
In my chest
Where my heart used to be.

So I'm here at your door

To say,

I want my heart back..

SPIRIT

The Dance of Shiva

Eyebrows singed
Nose blistered and red
Lips cracked and scorched

My kinetic soul stood still,
My body melted,
Mind and thoughts burned
Like torched paper.

What happened?

One tiny spark
Off the silver heels
Of the Eternal Dancer
Kissed me.

A Drunken Dragonfly

*I am the deep black ink
That keeps the stars afloat.
I am the endless cosmic night.*

*I am the life force of every living thing.
I am in your blood, your secret heart, your soul.
I am where your spirit goes at death.*

*I am the measure of wisdom, of compassion,
To whom all great religions call,
Though they've yet to speak*

My language well.

*I write the music of the spheres
And teach the birds to sing it.
I am your prayers answered.*

*Still, you do not know Me.
Won't catch My name on solar winds
Or hear My voice in ocean waves.*

*You're like a drunken dragonfly
That rips his wings off
While in the midst of sight*

*Wake up!
You're missing quite a show..*

The Red Shawl

From time
To time,
Quietly,
Disguised
As ordinary,
The spirit of peace
comes to call.

Wafts in
On sweet
Scented incense,

Shyly slips
A soft red shawl
Around my
Shoulders.

Then,
Just as I
Speak her name
(As would a startled sparrow)
Peace departs..

Last Night

In a dream
I heard the word
"Divest".

I watched my hand
Let go
Of all my
Worldly treasures
From my silver
Treasure chest.

Then, just before
Reaching for the door,
The door to eternity,

I saw myself stand naked,
Naked and luminous
With fantastic
Golden wings..

The Knower And The Known

*The great creator
Wished to know
The joy and pain
Of man,
So He created lovers.*

*Man wished to know
The mind and purpose
Of God,
So he fell in love..*

Soup Soul With Biscuits

What must be done
To be real?
What must be done
To be whole?

Simply this:
Be crushed by the weight
Of your own choices,
Wounded by
Endless labor.

Return to your private journey
One thousand times
only to fall
One thousand times more.

Marry you fiery heart
To your frigid intellect,
Sit down and eat
Your own raw soul.

Anything less
Isn't real,
Anything less
Isn't whole..

Why You Came

*You are
What you are here
To find.*

*You are
The treasure
You are seeking.*

*This crazy labyrinth
You're traveling
Leads only inward,*

*Where you may find
What you are here
To find..*

Meeting The Shadow

As he
Lingers in
The depths
Of soul
He meets
His fool,
His failure,
His sinner.

He walks awhile
Among them,
Hears their stories
Hears their lament,

Then grabs
The light
Of self-forgiveness
To fly up,
Up and out..

Madre De Las Estrellas

Santa Maria,
Cosmic feminine of celestial lands
Help her accept the abundant gifts
You have kindly placed in her hands.

Mother of the stars above
Let her feel your sweet blessings
Of gratitude and love.

Santa Maria,
May she be permitted
To forgive herself
For sins not committed.

Queen of time and space
Hold her up to the moon
That she may kiss
Its snowy face..

The Holy Spirit

I am the house of fire.
On I'll burn
As I do now,
Forever blazing.

I am not the owner
Of this flame
I am the space
For its existence.

Not blood
Flows through my veins
But fire,
That fire alone can cool
And yours alone..

The Wind Blows Through ME

Once I was a wolf
Once I was the sky
Once a willow tree.

Time moves
Forms change

Space stays
The same in me.
Sacred,
Starry
Wild
And wide.

Space stays
The same
In me..

Notes from the Borderlands

Some of us are wildish
We tear out all the pages
We only roam the borders
Hide the keys to all the cages.

We hear the angels chanting
Know the devil's voices
See the wound in all the wounded
Feel the grief of painful choices.

Some of us live wild
Grow in untamed ways
Love with hearts wide open
Sail uncharted days.

We run across scorched deserts
Dance the highest ledge.
Be careful how you touch us
We walk the sharpest edge.

Some of us know spirit
We dwell in sacred places
We are the shamans to the soul
We own the scars
Seared on our faces..

POLITICS

·

Glass Soldier

Sent out
In glory
And speeches

Returns home
In broken
Jagged pieces.

Why speak
Of such sorrow
You may ask,

Because we all
Are soldiers
Made of glass..

It Was Your Country

I know you've yet to find
The words
To hold the feelings.

So, let me say it for you.

The truth, the beauty
Of the dream
Was real to you.

You held the keys.
It was your country
You're now an empty
Clay container
Falling to the ground.

It's over.

The jackals have won.
Of course they won,
You didn't know
You were the enemy.

The blood is on the wall.
They're sucking on your bones
They're eating your children's future.
They used your dreams
That are now
Just a foolish memory.

You're no longer needed.
They wish you'd walk
Out into space
And disappear.

Ninety nine plus one
Now equals one.

So, have I said it right?
Have I said it well enough?.

Two Women

She said
No
To two
Yes
To one.

That's why
Her story sounds
So strange to you.

You said
No
To the wide high way
Yes
To the comfort train.

That's why
Your story sounds
So odd to her.

She chose
The call
Of unconscious wilderness
Not the lure
Of hearth and home.

That's why

She still discusses
The joy and cost
Of freedom
With a thousand angels
On the mountain's
Rocky edge..

Recession's Wedding

I'll buy the wine
I'll make the bread,

I'll wash the sheets
For the wedding bed

A grand day it will be,
The day we wed.

And you, my love,
Bring stones for soup..

Willing Inmates

You're never going
Where we have been

What we have seen
You'll never see

What we know
You can't imagine.

You may have more
But more is not enough.

Do you ever listen
To the wisdom on the wind?

Lift one foot
To follow your own path?

The prison bars
Around your mind
You've forged yourself.

Will a hundred lifetimes
Come and go
Before you simply
Open the door and
Leave the cell?.

Wrong Box

*Please don't put me
In your box.
It's not my box.
It's much too small,
My spirit's grown
To ten feet tall.*

*I won't fit in
A box at all.*

*If you feel you must
Rename me,
Label and contain me,
Then wrap me in
A bag with rocks,
Drop me in
The deepest river,
Or put me in a jail
With locks,
But please, and now I'm begging,
Please, don't put me
In a box.*

Severely Anemic

Your conversation is
Verbal cotton candy
Sticky, pink and fluffy
Dissolving into nothing
In my mouth.

Chewing on sweet air,
Gagging on spun sugar.

Tell me
Something real,
Something brief, or witty
A few nuggets
Of wisdom,
A morsel of truth.

It may not be
Grade A
But after talking with you
I feel the need
To tear into
A big chunk of
Red, raw meat..

Going Down Slow

Coming back
To where
I started
I remember
Why I left

This plush
Velvet prison,
This sea
Of bland tranquility,
Where all the rules
Are set.

I'm going down slow
In this bog
Of conventionality,
This subtle brutality

With not a soul
to save me..

ZEN

Buddha's Request

Boundless compassion?

I'm still busy
Climbing
The slippery, slimy
Tree Of self

Growing out of
The soupy swamp
Of Samsara.

Boundless compassion?

The very minute
I get out of
This damn tree..

Zen Again

We are always
At the present moment
The sum total
Of all our past decisions,
All our future dreams.

Ah, not so
Says the stranger.

We are always
The sum total
Of that quiet being
Who surely lives
In the presence
Of the ever present
Now..

A Flight of Hours

In the day
Before tomorrow,
In the year before
The next

Pay attention
To your hours
Or you may
Find yourself
In the desolate forest
Of pale memories

Where, if you dwell
Too long,
Time brings you to
The end of all tomorrows.

Pay close attention
To the hours
Of today,

For, unlike
Robins in spring,
They do not
Fly home again..

The Most Beautiful
Bird in the World

Could be you.

An ethereal spirit bird;
One wing of Wisdom,
One of Compassion.

You could fly
On the winds
Of pure kindness
Into the golden corona
Of the sacred sun.

But you will need
Both wings..

The Philosopher's Stone

When the odyssey
Is over,
All the tigers tamed,
When there is nothing left
To rail against
Except the wind,
The cold,
The seasons,

There is still
One lesson waiting
That can change lead
To stunning gold.

The lesson is
Forgiveness
The lesson is
The last,
And certainly
The deepest..

Trip to Nirvana

To reach nirvana
Go sit
With a cat
In your own
Backyard.

Passport,
Cool travel gear,
Hiking boots-
Not required.

Just the cat,
If that.

ETC

Perchance To Dream

Slowly slipping
Into the silent
Stream of sleep,
Sinking softly
Into quicksand
Half an acre deep.

Leaving sticky tangles
Far behind,
Towards the arms
Of vast unconscious bliss,
Letting go
The restless
Racing mind.

Traveling down
The edge
Of the indigo abyss.

Down, down
Once again
To kiss
The constant lover,
Sweet Morpheus..

La Loba

She is a wolf,
Wild sleek and grey
She hunts by night
She sleeps by day.

No one can catch her,
No one's as swift,
From one hill to another
She silently shifts.

You may see her at dawn,
At daybreaks first light,
A flash of wildness,
She's a dazzling sight.

There's dew on her coat,
Mud on her paws,
Blood on her mouth,
Meat in her jaws.

She is a wolf
Wild, sleek and grey
She hunts by night
She sleeps by day..

To An Old Love

Oh what a masquerade
I played to please you.

You left anyway.

I simply could have
Been myself,
Then, at least
You would be leaving

Me.

From Moon 'Til Morning

We sailed softly
Through the satin sky,
On towards the lemon moon.
Off starboard galaxies floated by
As we sang our sailor's tune.

By magenta morning
You were gone from me,
Slipped off into the night,
Now I wander alone
On this star-filled sea,
Adrift on this astral flight.

Sometimes I can just
Catch sight of you,
While you skim
The face of the sun.

I doubt we'll sail together again,
As I steer my ship of one.

Compass in hand,
Wind at my back,
I steer my ship of one..

Calling

Over here,
This small voice
Calling from a corner
Of the universe.

Over here,
Come find me.
I have a world of wondrous
Jewels in my pocket.

Come find me,
I'll share
Them all,
One by wondrous one
With you..

Under The Rug

The Chuckawalla
Baby Bite Choo man
Lived under the living room rug.

He was absolutely terrifying
Even though he was
The size of a bug.

He had long green teeth,
Blood red eyes,
Frequent raging fits.

One day the dog
Came galumphing by,
Smashed him all to bits.

Apparently a paw
Came crashing down,
Caught him in the neck.

Although it's been
A year since then,
His wife is still a wreck..

Mexico

Mexico, warm Mexico
Your sunsets glow,
Your colors .ow,
Your sweet winds blow.

I hear the whisper
Of the brown Madonna's song
The music of fiesta wafts along.

I love your high Sierra Madre
Your salty sensual sea.

Please, Mexico,
Save a little place for me..

New Mexico

Raw west winds
Sweep across
Wide mesas,
Exquisite sky,
The canopy.

Willful spirits
Rip through
Troops of juniper.
Only the deeply rooted
Stand.

All else
Long, long since
Blown away.

To the pleasure
Of the desert gods
Coyotes sing
Their crazy love song
To this fearsome beauty.

Such is my interior canvas;
A wide, clean-swept soul scape
In pale earth tones.

Yet, sometimes
In deepest sleep
I dream of cool,
Moist nights,
Soft mist rising
Off verdant fields.

How could I not?
When celtic rain runs with
Ancient memories
Through my blood..

No Chance

You are so firmly planted
In a world of force and logic,
Can you dare imagine
A translucent, subtle world
Of flow and light.

I find no way
To break you open
To the fantastic luminous
That so easily
Exists for me.

No chance
Of our worlds colliding.
We're not circling
The same sun..

Fool Moon

This big full moon
With its neon grin
Takes me by the throat
Lets the night witch in.

This blue full moon
Takes a hold of me
Won't set me free
Till the end of night.

That bright orb hanging
Keeps my brains clanging
Gets strange ghosts banging
Like some old barn doors.

This cool moon glow
With its ice blue light
Has its grip on me
Till the last of night.

Till dawn.